ABBIEISMS

Making life a little bit easier

First Printing: 2021

ISBN 978-1-8383912-0-1

Abbie Akinfenwa

United Kingdom

Contents

Introduction

Why read this book?

Why am I writing this book?

What do I want to get out of it?

What are Abbieisms?

How did the book on Abbieisms come about?

Chapter One – Looking After You

Why are you not looking after yourself?

Abbieisms on Looking After You

Chapter Two – Making Work Work

Abbieisms on Making Work Work

Chapter Three - Relationships

Chapter Four – Setting Goals

Qualities of a good goal

Abbieisms on Setting Goals

Chapter Five – Managing Finances

Abbieisms on Managing Finances

Abbieisms – The Conclusion

INTRODUCTION

Why read this book?

You are busy. Whether you are busy having a career, looking after kids, parents, community, life is just a long list of lists. This book is for people who like practical advice, but do not have a lot of time to go find it. People that are looking to embrace easy life hacks without major time investment.

You know there is a better way but you just haven't got the time to find it!

Abbieisms are for you! It is a quick read that gets to the point without excessive rambling.

If you are thinking to yourself, how can I make life simpler, how can I make life easier, how can I simplify my life, can it all be easier? This book is for you!

Its aim is to help you make life simpler, easier and give you tips for daily living. Make life work for you better than it currently is.

It is an easy read and you can read a particular chapter or the whole book at a go. The choice is yours.

This book will help you get what is important to you on your to-do list. Tackling the to-do list? I think that is the next book.

Why am I writing this book?

I have always had a knack for finding efficient ways of doing things. I am always looking for simple ways of getting things done without the drama. Anything that can help in making life a little bit easier, is my stock in trade.

I can take in a large amount of information and get to the salient points, quickly.

I am boringly practical and plain talking too. Over the last 20 years, I have acquired a common-sense approach to addressing things that has held me in good stead.

What do I want to get out of it?

My aim is to share my knowledge with the world in the quickest way possible.

If one person learns something from this book, then my job is done! My goal is to inspire, help and encourage my readers to look for simple ways of solving life's problems. If you use one of my tips? Good! If you share with a friend, even better!!!

What are Abbieisms?

To get to the root of *Abbieisms*, I will tell you a little bit about myself. My name is Abigail Akinfenwa, and everyone calls me Abbie. The only people who called me Abigail, were my parents when I was naughty or the reverend sisters at the Catholic boarding school I attended.

I read a lot and my natural inclination is always to find the quickest, easiest, most efficient way of doing things. I am someone who just gets on with it, whatever "it" is.

I have always been good with figures, understanding concepts quickly and completed my first university degree at 19.

I have a good friend from my university days, Ade. He is intelligent, easy going and we get on well. Over the years, we developed a habit of catching up to put the world to rights.

After one of our many "putting the world to rights" conversations, he commented on the nuggets of wisdom I always shared with him without the slightest inkling of how profound they were. We had a laugh about it and he said *"You and your Abbieisms"* Thereafter, anytime we talked, he would prompt me whenever I dropped an "*Abbieism*". I didn't really think anything of it and life continued, like it does.

How did the book on Abbieisms come about?

Fast forward a few decades in the Information Technology industry I decided that I wanted something different. I wanted a change. I wanted more flexibility, more control and a new challenge. I guess you could call it a "mid-life crisis". I had always been highly organised and efficient so being a virtual personal assistant appealed to me. Again, with my "efficiency hat" on, I thought, "what is the quickest way I can get going" and I decided to buy into a franchise. I researched franchise companies in that sector, interviewed a couple and found the one that matched my values and had the best rapport.

This was daunting to say the least, as I had spent the prior two decades as an employee.

As part of running this business, I upskilled myself in social media as I now have clients, for whom managing their social media accounts is part of the service I offer. I had advised my clients to post videos on *Facebook* because these got more reach than standard posts. I now had a dilemma, I had to practice what I preached. I needed to start doing videos myself.

I then remembered what Ade said about **Abbieisms** and thought, "That's it!". **Abbieisms** are practical tips which I use daily.

Doing the first video was nerve-wracking. I agonised for days, Should I? Shouldn't I? And then I thought "What is the worst that can happen?" My first video was viewed by over 300 people. I could not believe that people were interested! I had loads of comments and feedback and then started doing monthly postings. I put all my videos on Facebook and Youtube.

As I had said earlier, I love reading and over the years I have acquired a *Kindle*. It is a godsend. No more lugging books on holiday and wondering how to carry them all. I have downloaded so many books from *Kindle* why not create an e-book? Thus, I have condensed the contents of my videos, added a few more bits and created this e-book.

Once I sold the idea of the e-book to myself, I then reconsidered the format of publication as I do know some friends who do not have *Kindles* so *Kindle* plus book it is!

Eighteen months after starting my business, I was diagnosed with breast cancer. As I was relatively healthy, I didn't see this coming. I am not sure anyone does.

A year of surgery, chemotherapy and radiotherapy followed. This wake-up call gave me the momentum to get on with the book as the adage, life is short was a bit close to home.

The book on *Abbieisms* was born.

CHAPTER ONE
– LOOKING
AFTER YOU

'Look after yourself – there is only one you – La Reina'

'If I am not good to myself, how can I expect anyone else to be good to me – Maya Angelou'

Looking After You is one of my cardinal rules that I go to great pains to follow. You need to make sure you look after yourself otherwise you will not be able to look after anyone else. This means different things to different people. The key essence of this rule is ensuring your wellbeing is your priority. You may translate 'wellbeing' in different ways; psyche, essence, chi or sense of self, whatever language makes sense to you.

If you do not look after yourself, who are you expecting to look after you? If you are a child, your parents have that job. As an adult, you have that job for you.

Looking after you is imperative in maintaining your mental health and state of mind. Once they are in sync the rest follows. Mental health issues are on the rise in the UK and all over the world as people grapple with the multitude of things that come their way. 2020 saw the biggest pandemic in a 100 years with the Coronavirus. The whole world was affected.

Some people are good at looking after themselves. They are the lucky ones. Most people are so focused on the next big thing whether that is career advancement, monetary acquisition, or fame that they forget to look after themselves. Women are legendary at looking after everyone else to their detriment. Some women spend their day looking after their relatives, partners, friends, pets but completely forget about themselves.

Why are you not looking after yourself?

Why? Why? WHY???

1. *The (endless!) searching for perfection*
2. *Refusing to take shortcuts*
3. *Refusing to ask for help*
4. *Being a Martyr*
5. *I must do everything myself syndrome!*

The searching for perfection

In the world we live in, everyone strives for perfection. It is all around us, on the television, the internet, social media and advertising - the perfect job, hairstyle, boyfriend, girlfriend, career, children. Striving for perfection all the time is mentally exhausting. People expend so much energy to live in the perfect neighbourhood, have the right car, send the kids to the right school.

There is nothing wrong in aiming for improvement and making a better life. Where it gets tricky is when it causes you mental anguish. If doing something is causing you stress, you have a choice. There are not many things in life that one *has* to do, and you just may not feel you have the choice, but you do.

If your quest for perfection energises you then carry on but with most people that is not the case!

If it is okay to strive for perfection but listen to your body. Most of us may not recognise when we are stressed but our body does.

Refusing to take shortcuts

Is there a simpler way of getting something done? If there is then do that. Maybe you like a clean house but as well as having a full-time job and running after the kids, it is a distant memory.

You live by yourself and are never home as there is so much more to do outside your house.

You are in the sandwich generation, with kids and elderly parents to look after. There are never enough hours in the day!

Take a close look at your finances. If you can afford it, hire a cleaner, pay the kids extra pocket money to do their chores. Ask your partner. Decide on having the common living areas pristine and do not worry too much about the rest.

You do not like cooking, get a takeaway sometimes. Or when you do cook, cook a lot, and split into meal size portions and freeze it so you don't need to worry about it.

Cook simpler meals that do not require too many steps or take a lot of time. There are a lot of websites with simple recipes to draw from.

Can you delegate anything at a reasonable price and get someone else to do it? Or maybe barter the chores with someone else?

Refusing to ask for help

If you need help, ask! Do not suffer in silence. Sometimes this works out and sometimes it does not. What is the worst that can happen? You may be pleasantly surprised as you get help from where you least expected it. Maybe you do ask for help and do not get it, you are no worse off than you were before you asked so you have not lost anything. Maybe they can help next time, now they know it is something you struggle with.

Asking for help does not make you weak. Knowing your limitations and doing something about it makes you stronger not weaker.

Being a martyr

Do not think that you must do everything yourself and send yourself to an early grave trying to do it! You do not need to be a martyr. No-one wishes they had worked harder on their deathbed!

You do not get any brownie points for doing everything yourself. Most of the time, you end up with more to do, not less, or the halo effect is fleeting.

I must do everything myself

You may be agonising about something that you do not need to worry about. Why is this task so important to you but may not have as big an impact as you are expecting? This is your cue to drop it from your list or at least stop worrying about it!

Abbieisms on Looking After You

Is there anything more important? Human beings are complicated; body, mind and health are all one and the same. Looking after you requires looking after all facets not just your physical body.

What are my Abbieisms on looking after you?

a) Exercise
b) Eat Well
c) Listen to your body
d) Be Grateful and have a belief system

a) Exercise.

Find some form of exercise and do at least 3 times a week. Gym, Aerobics, Zumba, Pilates, Yoga, Swimming, Squash, Tennis, Walking, Dancing....there are endless forms of exercise. Find one you enjoy or at least one you can tolerate. Once those endorphins start cruising round you, you will begin to enjoy it.

The human body is a machine that needs a workout every so often. If you are a gym junkie and go to the gym every day, you are well on the way to looking after you.

Most people struggle to do any form of exercise. Take the stairs instead of the lift, park far away from the entrance of the cinema/supermarket, get off the bus/tube a stop early. All of these will increase your exercise levels.

If you could get yourself a fitness watch to measure how many steps you have done, even better!

Even if you do not enjoy the actual exercise, enjoy how you feel afterwards. I started running due to my cholesterol levels. The doctor gave me the option of increasing my cardio exercise and this was likely to reduce it and it worked. No need for medication. Side benefits are huge! I eat what I like, have a lot more energy, and it gives me time to think and I no longer have intestinal issues.

Do I like running? Not really but I like the side benefits, so I will continue... for now....

b) *Eat Well*

Do not worry about the latest food fad! Each year there is a new one. The simplest rule is everything in moderation. We already know fruit and vegetables tend to be better for you than pizza and cake. There is nothing wrong with the odd slice of pizza, but every day is probably not a good idea. We know that water will always be better than fizzy drinks or fruit juice and eating until you can eat no more is not good for anyone. None of these are fads and are just a good way to live.

You do not need a big rule book; good old common sense is usually enough unless you have allergies or any kind of medical condition that rules out certain foods. I advocate drinking water, eating loads of fruits and vegetables, manage your portion sizes and reduce your consumption of processed food. If you follow these, you are unlikely to go wrong.

c) *Listen to your body*

When you are feeling like everything is too much, take some time out.

Your body usually tells you when it has had enough if you take the time to listen to it.

Find something to recharge your batteries at least once a month. It could be the cinema to see a cheesy movie, or a comedy where you laugh so hard your eyes water, going to the theatre. You could meet up with friends for a meal, a show or if you are incredibly lucky, a holiday - whatever floats your boat.

It could be a massage, a spa visit, meditation, or prayer worship. I love getting massages and nowadays there are loads of promotions via companies that you can sign up to. Groupon and Wowchers are some examples of these types of services. There is always a way if you keen to find one.

During the pandemic of 2020, virtual activities flourished. It could be something virtual like bingeing on Netflix and Amazon Prime, doing online quizzes, cookery classes, there are so many options...

Find whatever it takes to help you relax and make sure you do.

d) Be Grateful and have a belief system

Be grateful for what you have and capable of doing. There will always be someone you are better off than.

Be grateful for what you perceive as the little things.

You wake up in the morning, not everyone did.

You have a car; the air-conditioning is on the fritz and it is 25^0C outside but it is better than having to take the bus.

You do not have a Mercedes, but it could be worse.

You would like a bigger house, but you are not homeless. You would like to eat out more often, but you have food.

I mentioned earlier on, my Catholic boarding school as a child, I am a practicing Catholic, so I would I say a prayer every morning to thank God for keeping me at night. It is the least I can do. I am not advocating you all become Christians, but a belief system, whatever that is, gives you some resilience to deal with the knocks life throws at you.

Meditation and reflection are good for making you pause. A lot of people do these on a regular basis and find them calming.

Chapter One - Recap

This chapter is giving you some **Abbieisms** about looking after yourself. If you do not look after yourself, you will not have anything for anyone else, so it is key that you do.

I hope it has given you some food for thought to recognise why you may not be looking after you.

Are you looking after yourself?

Do you do any exercise?

Are you aware of what you eat?

Do you listen to your body?

How is your mind?

What are you grateful for?

There are no wrong answers.

Answer these questions in your own time to help you identify what you will do next.

CHAPTER TWO
– MAKING
WORK WORK

How do you make work work? It is an eternal question. We all need to feel useful and needed. If you do not have some form of work, you will always be searching. Work does not have to be paid or you do not have to be an employee, it can be voluntary, non-profit or your business. It does not matter, what. As human beings, we must have a purpose, whatever that is.

Work provides a focus, a purpose and in most cases, a roof over your head. Even if you do not care about being needed or wanted, you need to fill your day doing something, so why not something that contributes to the world in some little way?

We cannot all be Bill Gates or Richard Branson who are excessively big influencers, but everyone has capacity to do great things when motivated.

You need to have a reason to get up in the morning,

especially on those mornings that you really do not want to. Most people want to feel needed.

Abbieisms on Making Work Work

a) Work at what you like

If you have a talent that you like and can earn a living doing it, then you are fortunate. It is a luxury that not many people have. It will be no hardship as you enjoy what you are doing. But for the need to earn a crust you would do it for free. 9 times of 10, if you like doing it and are good at it, it will make money.

You would work long hours and go the extra mile because you like what you do and get a buzz from doing it. If only that buzz could be bottled and sold....

If you recognise someone is good at something, you are more likely to hire them as their passion is infectious and attracts people to them as that skill shines through without effort.

We all know that one person that does certain things are effortlessly. They have an innate ability for the skill and just get on with it with little effort. It is that friend who has you over for dinner and cooks five courses in no time. They love what they do and would probably do it for free. They are your go-to person for new recipes and they are always experimenting. If that person told you they were opening a catering business, you would be their first customer as you already know they loved cooking and are good at it. You would also promote them at every opportunity.

That is the kind of talent I am talking about. Some people have it without seeming like they are applying little effort, but you all know it when we see it.

The same applies for students or people in the voluntary or charity sector, if you like what you are doing, you will be good at it and inspire others too.

If you can earn a living doing something you love and are good at, grab the opportunity with both hands!

b)   *Work at what you are good at*

This is the next best thing. You may not like a thing, but if you happen to be good at it, then use that. Do not let that talent go to waste. Utilise it in your work journey somehow.

These people may not have the passion of the people who love what they are doing but they are clearly above average in whatever it is they do. They are highly competent with that talent even though they may not love it.

If you fit in that camp, that is also good because as over time, you may even grow to like it. If you do not, it is not a deal breaker, that is not an issue. If you do it better than the next person, you are doing well.

When I set up my business, I realised it was about doing a good job that counted. Once you did a good job and started getting clients, they would tell other clients and the business will grow. The same applies when working in the corporate world, if you are good at your job, it shows and gets rewarded.

c)   *Get better if (a) or (b) do not apply*

Do you feel that you have no special skills or passions? Are you yearning for a better life? Do you feel you are not fulfilling your potential?

Your next option is to upskill yourself so at least you improve your current circumstance.

Nowadays, there is a lot of online training, so you do not need to leave one job to train for another. You can start a business while you are in a full-time job. Basically, make yourself better at something and then you will grow to love it.

You can find a mentor or coach to help you navigate whatever path you are trying to choose.

Constantly complaining about your life and not doing anything to move it forward will not change your current situation. If you keep doing what you are doing, you will keep getting what you are getting.

d)   *You are content so be the best you can be at whatever you do.*

You have heard that saying "anything that is worth doing, is worth doing   well".

You may not love what you do or be very good at it but you do it to the best of your ability.

Then you will have no regrets.

Last resort play the lottery. Someone has to win it and you never know, it could be you. And if it is – remember where you got the tip.

Chapter Two - Recap

In this chapter we started to look at making work work. How do you make work work for you?

What do you do for work? Are you happy doing it?

Are you naturally talented in what you do?

Are you good at what you do and recognised as such?

If you are not happy doing it, what will you do about it?

What is stopping you from doing something about it?

Are you content with what you do?

There are no wrong answers.

Answer these questions in your own time to help you identify what next.

CHAPTER THREE
- RELATIONSHIPS

Relationships are funny things. Human beings are social animals, we like to interact with others.

I read a poem recently by Benjamin Zephaniah, 'People need people'. It summarises all the things we like to do with people. Laugh with and at, cry with, please, tease, fight the list goes on. If you have a chance, google the full poem.

This poem clearly sums up why we need relationships, as we always want to share things with other people. You saw something funny today, you cannot wait to tell people. Even in today's world of social media, people still need people.

All relationships are important and feed into future relationships. This is why psychiatrists ask about family history, as the relationships you have growing up affect your mindset and behaviour patterns as you grow older.

In this context, I am referring to relationships that go beyond exchanging Christmas and birthday cards. I would consider those acquaintances. You need those too but a few good relationships are priceless.

Another quote I heard recently was ' If you want good friends, be a good friend.'

Maya Angelou summed it up 'I've learned that people will forget what you said, they will forget what you did, but they will never forget how you made them feel'.

Relationships are all about feelings and how we interact with each other and how we make each other feel.

There are different kinds of relationships that you may find yourself in at different stages in life:

You are the mentor or role model

This could be where you are the parent, older relative, boss, peer and the person in the relationship with you is on the receiving end. Your role in the relationship is to provide guidance, assistance, support, encouragement, and behaviour to emulate. For whatever reason, your opinions or views are respected, and the receiver looks up to you. Sometimes, the receiver may put you on a pedestal and admire things about you.

This is a precious relationship, as you have an opportunity to directly impact someone else's life. Be careful of your actions and advice, as in this relationship, you are looked at as a sage.

These relationships can sometimes be fraught as being mere human beings, we may end up shattering the receiver's illusions.

You are the mentee

This could be where you are the child, subordinate or younger person in a relationship with someone that you look up to. It could be in a work, familial or friend capacity. Usually, in this relationship, there is something you admire about the person and sometimes hero worship. You look at this person as having more knowledge or wisdom than you and look to them for advice and guidance. Again, as per the other relationship, the mentor could end up not living up your lofty ideals as they are only human.

You are partners

This would be significant other. This could be a husband, wife, long term partner, girlfriend, or boyfriend. This relationship is probably the one with the most angst associated with it, as sometimes expectations exist that may not be voiced but cause resentment when not met.

When a partnership works, it can be life changing. You support each other, finish each other's sentences, you are one unit against the world.

You are peers

You may not be of the same age group, but the relationship is less of a mentor or mentee. You could be partners, siblings, friends, or work colleagues who through various encounters have developed mutual respect. You would socialise, converse and exchange views and opinions.

Relationships can morph through these stages. As an example, you could start out as a peer and then become a mentor as life changes and events occur. The same person can be a mentor and a mentee. It is all a matter of perspective and fluidity of relationships.

Abbieisms on Relationships

Regardless of the type of relationship, it should help you develop.

A relationship should make you a better person, either so you can be an example to someone else or to make someone else proud of you. It is why a child seeks the parents' approval and sibling rivalry can stimulate healthy competition.

Relationships are there for support and encouragement.

Relationships must maintain some equilibrium. Relationships should be beneficial for both parties. Comfort, love, support, encouragement. Someone to cry with, laugh with or at or even to shout at.

Both parties must get something out of the relationship, otherwise resentment sets in. Respect and trust are key in nurturing relationships. Compromise also plays a part.

Relationships should have more ups than downs.

Is the relationship healthy or toxic?

You do not need a relationship that makes you feel bad about yourself.

'No one can make you feel inferior without your consent' – Eleanor Roosevelt

You do not need a relationship that makes you feel small or belittles you in any way.

You do not need a relationship where you have to be overly cautious anout what you say and do all the time.

You do not need a relationship that makes you question why you are in that relationship.

You always have a choice, although it may not seem like it. When you are in a disastrous relationship, it is sometimes hard to see the wood from the trees.

Having one healthy relationship is better than having ten meaningless ones. When it comes to relationships Quality trumps Quantity any day.

Chapter Three - Recap

In this chapter we have looked at the different types of relationships and how you can tell if a relationship is not necessarily working for you.

Examine your relationships.

Are they making you grow?

Do you both benefit from the relationship?

Is the relationship working for you?

Do you need to build new relationships?

There are no wrong answers.

Answer these questions in your won time to help you identify where you are with your relationships.

CHAPTER FOUR – SETTING GOALS

Goals can be scary. Goals can make you feel empowered or can make you feel constrained.

Goals are important to help give you some focus in what you are doing with your life.

Some goals are imposed on you. As an example, if you buy a car on a 3-year payment plan, the goal is you will pay off the loan at rate $x\%$ over 3 years. There are penalties if you do not.

Another example could be attending a course. Most courses are for a defined period and are expected to be completed in that timeframe.

What I am referring to in this chapter are goals that you set yourself.

The attainment of a goal should make a difference in your life. It should give you a sense of fulfilment and make you proud of yourself.

Qualities of a good goal

What are the qualities of a good goal?

Is just getting up in the morning achieving a goal? It depends on your starting point. If you have been going through addiction or trauma and not able to get up in the morning, that may be a goal for you. It all depends on your starting point.

Some of you may have heard of the *SMART* technique. This is a brilliant way of assessing whether the goal you are planning on has been thought through sufficiently.

S – Specific

Need to be able to articulate what the goal is.

M – Measurable

You can measure how much has been done.

A – Achievable

You are capable of doing the goal.

R – Relevant

What does achieving the goal mean to you? Why are you doing this goal? If it is not relevant, you will not focus on it.

T – Timely.

There is a timeframe associated with it.

I will use an example to illustrate.

I want to publish a book. This is specific (ish), measurable (it is written or isn't), achievable (depends on the book), relevant (could be) and not timely.

I want to publish a book before the end of 2020. This is now timely but could be more specific as to the type of book to assess how realistic or achievable it is.

A revised SMART target could be:

'I want to publish a five-chapter self-help book by the end of 2020 to spread my knowledge on a range of topics to a wider audience.'

Specific - I know the type of book.

Measurable - you could count the chapters

Achievable - I have experience of self-help books and now has a time frame associated with

Relevant – I have a clear purpose why

Timely – by the end of 2020

This is much clearer and will be easier to monitor how progress is being made.

It is specific – self-help book rather than an unspecified genre.

It is measurable – 5 chapters so when I have done 3 chapters I will be 60% of the way there.

It is achievable – I have expertise in self-help books.

It is relevant – there is a purpose for doing it.

It is Timely – There is a timeframe attached to it.

Conversely if I set a target of

'I want to publish a five-chapter book on nuclear physics in a years' time'.

It is specific.

It is measurable from the number of chapters.

It is not achievable, as I have no knowledge of nuclear physics

It is not relevant, as I am unlikely to have a deep connection with nuclear physics overnight. I will not acquire enough knowledge of nuclear physics to write a book in the time frame given.

It is timely as there is a time limit assigned to it.

Looking at the problem in reverse - what do you think happens when you have no goals? Well, I hate to surprise you; but this is never actually the case. All that happens is it you don't consciously set goals, a set of unconscious goals set in and guide you. And almost unfailingly, the goals will simply be to give you the maximum pleasure, minimum stress, and least effort – right NOW.

Completely disregarding next year, next month or even tomorrow. Chilling on the sofa, tub of chocolate ice cream. Large glass of wine or huge pile of chips; feels so good now. And unless you have concrete goals that this lifestyle impacts; that's how it will go.

In a game of football, you can be the player; or you

can be the ball. Your choice.

Too many defenders – (excessive focus of stopping bad things from happening over positively making good things happen) – leads to feelings of being deprived of things rather than going out to achieve and being grateful (see earlier).

Abbieisms on Setting Goals

You should have them written somewhere, your phone, pinned on the fridge, whatever works for you. Some people like vision boards. Having the goal in your line of vision helps your subconscious tune into it more. Have you ever considered buying something? Lets say a red car. Once that is planted in your head, you will be constantly seeing red cars. They have always been there; you are just more attuned to them.

They stop you from drifting. You have an idea of what you want to happen, as opposed to life happening to you.

They give you a warm glow when you have achieved them. Therefore, the relevance is important. If it is not relevant to you, you will lose focus.

They give you a focus and structure.

You should aim for short, mid and long-term goals.

Once you have your goals, you can then split the goal into achievable bits of work which need to be included in your daily tasks. A goal without a plan is a dream. I feel another book coming on...

Goals change. They are not fixed as life changes too. It is okay to change them as you grow, and opportunities arise.

Chapter Four – Goals Recap

In this chapter, we have looked at goal setting and why these may be important.

Do you have goals?

Do you have them written down somewhere?

If you do not have goals, do you think you need them?

What do you dream of that you are yet to achieve in reality?

Why do you think that is?

Start with six-month, one year, three years and then five year goals.

There are no wrong answers.

Answer these questions in your own time to help you identify where you are.

CHAPTER FIVE – MANAGING FINANCES

Money is a funny thing. We spend a lot of time thinking of how to acquire it, how to spend it and looking after it. We forget that money was invented for us, not the other way around.

We need a certain amount of money to pay bills and to live. The key to making money work for you is understanding its value. The same logic applies whether you have £100 or £10,000.

Having a few guidelines that you can stick to, will make your relationship with money smoother.

Abbieisms on Managing Finances

a) *Have a budget*

A budget is your first good habit on the road to money management.

The Oxford dictionary defines a budget as an estimate of income and expenditure for a specific period. If you have looked at your earnings of £1,000 a month then a budget of £500 a month for rent leaves £500 for travel, food, gas, electricity, phone and everything else.

b) *Live within your means*

The whole point of a budget is to help you manage what you spend and making sure you fit within it. Living within your means is not exceeding your income with expenditure. If you live within your means, the odd bump in the road can be managed. If you live above your means, you are creating the bump in the road on a permanent basis. This is incredibly stressful.

If you rent a house that is £600 a month and you have a budget of £500, you have gone over your budget and will struggle to make ends meet each month.

c) *Look after the pennies*

Your spending habits should not morph with the amount of money you have. If you cultivate good habits when you have £100, those habits will hold true when you have £1,000.

The principle of managing money is the same regardless of the number of zeroes after the figures.

Know how much things cost and where your money goes. Some people feel that they should only bother to look after their money when they have a lot of it. A lot of times this inability to manage the smaller sums of money inhibits their getting the bigger amounts.

d) Get multiple streams of income

You will probably have a main source of income such as your work or business that brings in the lion-share of your income. If you have a side-line, such as shares that pay dividends or a com-mission-based activity of some sort, this will in-crease your income from time to time.

The best means of extra income is passive in-come. This is typically an investment that does not require face time but returns an income. Maybe you have written an online course, have a rental property, a book or multi-level marketing opportunity.

Savings are good, but investment is what makes your money grow.

e) Making large purchases

Shop around, do your homework and make sure you know what a good, average or low price for the item you are buying.

Haggle! Some shops will give you a discount if pay-ing cash or if purchasing multiple items. Haggling is not a dirty word. My husband cringes when I ask for money off when I go to department stores but a lot of the time, I get something.

When purchasing online, leave in your basket overnight. Some retailers will send you a discount code.

Sleep on it, if you can so you have a clear head about what you are buying.

f) Get value

That sofa that costs £20 less but took two hours round trip to pick it up plus petrol would have been cheaper to pay the extra £20 and have it delivered directly to your house. By the time you add your petrol and time, it is not as cheap as first imagined.

Some people will drive to three different food stores because some items are cheaper in one than the other. Unless you are driving past anyway, going to three shops to buy food is not cheaper.

You could buy a £20 pair of shoes that would last you three months whilst a £50 pair of leather shoes may be more expensive but will last longer. Invest in quality that lasts.

Know how much items cost so you get value for money as opposed to cheap things.

g) Review your expenditure and outgoings periodically.

Review your spending at least once a year. Are you spending too much on certain items? Can you get the same quality for less money? In the UK, phone companies always have offers, so it is worth changing your provider from the time to time. The same goes for gas and electricity. Do you need that cable subscription, Netflix and Amazon Prime when you hardly watch them? Maybe not.

That magazine subscription that is renewed automatically, or that tool you downloaded and used once? Be intentional with what you spend and where you spend it.

h) Debt is not a bad thing

If debt is managed, it is not a bad thing. Some purchases allow 0% interest. If you had a £1,000 for a new sofa and you invested that in something that paid 5% you could get the sofa and pay it off and make a profit. You may be starting a business and borrow some of the money to minimise the risk to yourself. The key is manageable, affordable debt not out of control debt with high interest charges.

i) Have Emergency savings

You need at least two months' income as easy to assess savings. This will cover the car breaking down, a leaky roof or any emergency that arises. This way you are not borrowing each time something happens.

Unfortunately, in life, these things happen and if you have no savings will constantly be a source of angst.

Chapter Five – Finance Recap

This chapter is about giving you tools to build a healthy relationship with money.

Do you have a budget?

Do you know how much you earn?

Do you know how much you spend?

What is your attitude towards money?

When have you last reviewed what you earn versus what you spend?

There are no wrong answers.

Answer these questions in your own time to assess where you are with your finances.

Abbieisms – The Conclusion

I have given you a brief glimpse of my philosophy, my **Abbieisms** that have helped me make life easier for me. I hope the book gives you enough food for thought and goes some way to making life easier for you too.

It is filled with tips for living that are not onerous to incorporate but can pay big dividends. The idea is to give you easy ways for a simpler life, life hacks and tips for living to make life simpler, easier, and less stressful all round.

Make life work for you as best you can.

Now for a quick recap...

Chapter One was Looking After You. Are you looking after you? Is there more you can do for this to become what you do by default as opposed to when you get stressed?

Chapter Two is about Making Work Work. Is work working for you? Do you hop out of bed in the morning raring to go? Or are up at 2am worrying about how bad the next day will be or buzzing with ideas that you cannot wait to start?

Chapter Three is about Relationships. Are your relationships working? Are you the mentor or mentee? How do these relationships make you feel?

Chapter Four is about Setting Goals. Have you set any goals? Did you monitor them? Are they important to you?

Chapter Five is about Managing Finances. Having clear guidelines of how you manage your finances will give you a healthier relationship with it.

I hope you have learnt something in each chapter, or it has given you some food for thought to examine things you could do to make your life simpler.

Thank you again for reading this book and I hope you found some *Abbieisms* that resonated with you and will help you in your day-to-day life.

I look forward to sharing more books with you in the future.

Share this book with someone else, buy it as a present and *if you could leave a review for me on Amazon that would be greatly appreciated!*

If you purchased a paperback, please send any feedback or reviews to abbieisms@abbieisms.co.uk.

Till the next book!

Printed in Great Britain
by Amazon

59941894R00031